William H

CW01023859

By United Library

https://campsite.bio/unitedlibrary

Table of Contents

Disclaimer

This biography book is a work of nonfiction based on the public life of a famous person. The author has used publicly available information to create this work. While the author has thoroughly researched the subject and attempted to depict it accurately, it is not meant to be an exhaustive study of the subject. The views expressed in this book are those of the author alone and do not necessarily reflect those of any organization associated with the subject. This book should not be taken as an endorsement, legal advice, or any other form of professional advice. This book was written for entertainment purposes only.

Introduction

Discover the extraordinary life of William Howard Taft, the 27th President of the United States and the only person to have served as both President and Chief Justice of the Supreme Court. Taft's journey, from his birth in Cincinnati, Ohio, in 1857 to his death in 1930, is a fascinating tale of ambition, politics, and judicial legacy.

Raised in a family of political prominence, Taft's career was marked by a series of extraordinary achievements. From his early days as a judge to his appointment as Governor of the Philippines and then as Secretary of War under President Roosevelt, Taft's rise to power was swift and impressive.

As President, Taft navigated a tumultuous political landscape, facing challenges from within his own party and across the nation. His presidency was marked by his efforts to navigate international affairs, especially in East Asia and Latin America, as well as his attempts to reform trade tariffs and address conservation and antitrust issues.

Taft's history is an example of dedication and service to his country, culminating in his appointment as Chief Justice, where his conservative views on business and advances in individual rights left a lasting impact on the nation's legal landscape.

Discover the legacy of one of America's most intriguing leaders in this fascinating biography of William Howard Taft.

William Howard Taft

William Howard Taft (Cincinnati, September 15, 1857-Washington, D. C., March 8, 1930) was the twenty-seventh President of the United States (1909-1913) and the tenth Chief Justice of the Supreme Court (1921-1930). He is the only person in U.S. history to have held both offices.

He was born in 1857 in Cincinnati into the Taft family, which had a long tradition of power in the United States. His father, Alphonso Taft, was a prominent Republican politician, who served as Secretary of War and Attorney General of the United States. William Taft received his law degree from Yale University. Before becoming president, Taft was elected to serve on the Cincinnati Supreme Court in 1887. In 1890 he was appointed solicitor general of the United States and in 1891 a judge of the 6th Circuit Court of Appeals. In 1901 President William McKinley appointed him governor general of the Philippines, in 1904 Secretary of War by then President Theodore Roosevelt and in 1906 temporary governor of Cuba at the request of the president of Cuba, Tomás Estrada Palma, to avoid an internal war in the country between different political tendencies.

With Roosevelt's help, Taft had little opposition to the Republican nomination for president in 1908 and easily defeated William Jennings Bryan for the presidency in the November election. Educated at Yale, he was elected in 1909 for president of the United States, succeeding Roosevelt. During his term Congress approved two important amendments: the sixteenth, by which taxes could be collected by deducting them directly from income, and the seventeenth, by which senators could be directly elected.In October of that same year, he granted two interviews: the first in El Paso, Texas and the last one in Ciudad Juárez, held at the border customs office, located on 16 de Septiembre Avenue, thus being the first interviews made in the southern border of the United States and in Mexico, when making a state visit to the then Mexican President Porfirio Díaz. Likewise, during the government of Francisco I. Madero he had complaints regarding the threats of Ambassador Henry Lane Wilson, who supported General Victoriano Huerta in consummating his treason. Years later he also met Mexican President Plutarco Elías Calles.

In the White House, he focused on East Asian rather than European affairs and repeatedly intervened to support or overthrow Latin American governments. Taft sought reductions in trade tariffs , then a major source of government revenue, but the resulting bill was heavily influenced by special interests. His administration was fraught with conflict between the conservative wing of the Republican Party, with which Taft was often sympathetic, and its progressive wing, toward which Roosevelt increasingly moved. Roosevelt challenged Taft for reelection in 1912. Taft used his control of the party machine to win a bare majority of delegates and Roosevelt broke with the party. The split left Taft with little chance of a reelection, and he carried only Utah and Vermont against Woodrow Wilson's victory in the 1912 election.

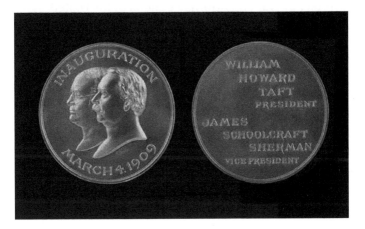

Biography

First years

William Howard Taft was born on September 15, 1857, in Cincinnati, Ohio, the son of Alphonso Taft and Louise Torrey. The Taft family was not particularly wealthy and lived in a modest home in the suburb of Mount Auburn. Alphonso served as a judge and ambassador, and was also Secretary of War and Attorney General of the United States under President Ulysses S. Grant.

William Taft was not considered a bright child, but he was a tireless worker; his parents who were quite demanding motivated him and his four siblings to achieve success, accepting nothing less. He attended Woodward High School in Cincinnati. At Yale University, where he entered in 1874, the robust and jovial Taft was popular and excelled as a champion wrestler in the heavyweight category in student competitions. A classmate claimed that he achieved his successes through effort and dedication rather than being the smartest, and that he always maintained his integrity. He was accepted as a member of Skull and Bones, the Yale secret society co-founded by his father. He is one of three U.S. presidents, along with George H W Bush and George W. Bush, who belonged as members of this society. In 1878, Taft graduated second in his class out of 121 students. He attended Cincinnati Law School, graduating with a law degree in 1880. While in law school, he worked on *The Cincinnati Commercial* newspaper, edited by Murat Halstead. Taft was assigned to cover news in the local courts and also spent his free time reading law books in his father's office; both activities gave him a working knowledge of the law that was not taught in the classroom. Shortly before graduating from law school, Taft went to Columbus to take the bar exam and passed easily.

Ohio Judge

After his admission, Taft devoted himself full time to his job at *Cincinnati Commercial*. Halstead was willing to hire him permanently at a higher salary if he would forego further study, but Taft refused. In October 1880, Taft was appointed deputy prosecuting attorney for Hamilton County and took office the following January. He resigned in January 1882 after President Chester A. Arthur appointed him as collector of internal revenue for the first district of Ohio, an area centered in Cincinnati.Taft refused to fire competent employees who were not favored politically and ended up resigning as collector in March 1883, he wrote to President Arthur that he wished to begin his private practice in Cincinnati. In 1884, Taft campaigned for the Republican candidate for president,

Maine Senator James G. Blaine, who lost to New York State Governor Grover Cleveland.

In 1887, Taft, then 29, was appointed to a vacancy on the Cincinnati Superior Court by Governor Joseph B. Foraker. The appointment was good for just over a year, after which he would have to face the voters, and in April 1888 he ran for election for the first time in his life. He was elected for a full five-year term. Some two dozen of Taft's opinions as a state judge survive, the most significant being *Moores & Co. v. Bricklayers' Union No. 1* (1889) if only because it was used against him when he ran for president in 1908. The case involved several construction workers who refused to work for any firm that dealt with a company called *Parker Brothers*, with which they were in dispute. Taft ruled that the union's action amounted to a secondary boycott, which was illegal.

Marriage

It is unclear when Taft met Helen Herron, often called Nellie, but it was not until later in 1880, when she mentioned in her diary that she had received an invitation from him to a party. By 1884, they were meeting regularly and in 1885, after an initial rejection, she agreed to marry him. The wedding took place at the Herron home on June 19, 1886. William Taft remained faithful to his wife throughout the nearly 44 years of their marriage. Nellie Taft pushed her husband as hard as her parents had, and could be very outspoken with her criticism. The couple had three children, of whom the eldest, Robert, became a U.S. senator.

Attorney General of the United States

There was a vacancy on the U.S. Supreme Court in 1889, and Governor Foraker suggested that President Harrison appoint Taft to fill it. Taft was 32 years old and his career goal had always been a seat on the Supreme Court. He actively sought the appointment, writing to Foraker to urge him to press his case, while telling others that he was unlikely to get it. Instead, in 1890 he was appointed Solicitor General of the United States by then-President Benjamin Harrison. When Taft arrived in Washington in February 1890, the office had been vacant for two months and work was piling up. He worked to eliminate the backlog, while simultaneously educating himself about federal law and procedures that he had not previously needed as an Ohio state judge.

New York Senator William M. Evarts, former Secretary of State, had been a classmate of Alphonso Taft's at Yale. Evarts called to see his friend's son as soon as Taft took office, and William and Nellie Taft were introduced to Washington high society. Nellie Taft was ambitious; it bothered her that the people Taft socialized with were mainly Supreme Court justices, rather than the arbiters of

Washington society such as Theodore Roosevelt, John Hay, Henry Cabot Lodge and their wives.

In 1891, Taft introduced a new policy: "confession of error," whereby the U.S. government would concede a Supreme Court case that it had won in the lower court but that the solicitor general thought it should have lost. At Taft's request, the Supreme Court reversed a murder conviction that Taft said had been based on inadmissible evidence. The policy continues to this day.

Although Taft was successful as Solicitor General, winning 15 of the 18 cases he argued before the Supreme Court, he was pleased when, in March 1891, the U.S. Congress created a new judgeship for each of the U.S. Courts of Appeals and Harrison appointed him to the Sixth Circuit, based in Cincinnati. In March 1892, Taft resigned as solicitor general to resume his judicial career.

Judge of the Court of Appeals (1892-1900)

Taft's appointment as a federal judge was for life, which could open the door to a possible promotion to the Supreme Court. His older half-brother, Charles, who was successful in business, supplemented Taft's government salary, which allowed him, his wife Nellie, and their family to live comfortably. Taft's duties involved presiding over trials in the circuit, which encompassed Ohio, Michigan, Kentucky, and Tennessee, and collaborating with

Supreme Court Justice John Marshall Harlan, the circuit judge, and other Sixth Circuit judges in appellate review. During this period, from 1892 to 1900, Taft experienced great personal and professional satisfaction.

According to some historians Taft's figure has not been as conservative as he is made out to be, "While Taft shared the fears about the social unrest that dominated the middle classes during the 1890s, he was not as conservative as his critics believed. He supported the right of workers to organize and strike, and ruled against employers in several negligence cases." Among these was *Voight v. Baltimore & Ohio Southwestern Railway Co.* Taft's decision for a worker injured in a railroad accident violated the contemporaneous doctrine of freedom of contract and was later overturned by the Supreme Court. On the other hand, the Taft verdict in *United States v. Addyston Pipe and Steel Co.* was unanimously affirmed by the high court. Taft's opinion, in which he held that an association of pipe manufacturers had violated the Sherman Antitrust Act, was described by Henry Pringle, his biographer, as "definitely and specifically revived."

In 1896, Taft became dean and professor of property at his *alma mater*, Cincinnati Law School, a position that required him to prepare and deliver two-hour lectures each week.He was dedicated to his law school and deeply committed to legal education, introducing the case method into the curriculum.As a federal judge, Taft could not get involved in politics, but he followed it closely, being a supporter of the Republicans. He watched with some incredulity as Ohio Governor William McKinley's campaign unfolded in 1894 and 1895, writing "*I can find no one in Washington who wants him.*" By March 1896, Taft realized that McKinley would probably be nominated and did not support him at first. He landed solidly in McKinley's campaign after former Nebraska Representative William Jennings Bryan in July of that year was elected by the 1896 Democratic National Convention with his Cross of Gold speech. Taft feared that people would hoard gold in anticipation of a Bryan victory, but he could do nothing but worry. McKinley was elected; when a seat opened on the Supreme Court in 1898, the only one to open under McKinley's presidency, the president appointed Joseph McKenna.

From the 1890s until his death, Taft played an important role in the international legal community. He was active in many organizations, was a leader in the world arbitration movement, and taught international law at Yale Law School. Taft advocated the establishment of a world court of arbitration supported by an international police force and is considered an important proponent of the "world peace through law" movement. One of the reasons for his break with Roosevelt in 1910 was Roosevelt's insistence that arbitration was a naive policy and that only war could decide major international disputes.

Governor of the Philippines (1900-1902)

In January 1900, Taft was called to Washington by President William McKinley. Taft had aspired to be appointed to the Supreme Court, but instead the president proposed that he serve on the commission charged with organizing a civilian government in the Philippines. The president assured him that if he fulfilled this task, he would be appointed to the next vacancy on the high court. Taft accepted and was appointed head of the commission, sailing for the islands in April 1900. At that time the United States was engaged in the Philippine-American War in which the Filipinos were demanding their independence.

The Filipinos were fighting for their independence, but the U.S. forces, led by the military governor, General Arthur MacArthur Jr. had the upper hand in the year 1900. Although General MacArthur was reluctant to cooperate with members of the commission he was forced to cooperate with Taft, since McKinley had given the commission control of the islands' military budget. The commission assumed executive power in the Philippines on September 1, 1900; on July 4, 1901, Taft became civilian governor. MacArthur, until then military governor, was relieved by General Adna Chaffee, who was appointed alone as commander of U.S. forces. As governor general, Taft oversaw the final months of the primary phase of the Philippine-American war. He approved General James Franklin Bell's use of concentration camps in the provinces of Batangas and Laguna, and accepted the surrender of Philippine General Miguel Malvar on April 16, 1902. In February 1902, Taft testified before the Senate on the Philippines regarding alleged crimes committed by the U.S. Marine Corps against Filipino civilians; he admitted that the Marines had committed some crimes, such as torture, but denied any connection with Bell's concentration camps.

Taft saw Philippine independence as decades away from happening. Many Americans in the Philippines viewed the locals as racially inferior, but Taft wrote shortly before his arrival, "*We propose to banish this idea from their minds*. Taft did not enforce racial segregation at official events and treated Filipinos as social equals. Nellie Taft recalled that "*neither politics nor race should influence our hospitality in any way.*"

McKinley was assassinated in September 1901 and was succeeded by Theodore Roosevelt. Taft and Roosevelt first became friends around 1890, when Taft was attorney general and Roosevelt a member of the U.S. Civil Service

Commission. Taft, after McKinley's election, urged Roosevelt's appointment as undersecretary of the Navy and watched Roosevelt become a war hero, governor of New York and vice president of the United States. They were reunited when Taft went to Washington in January 1902 to recover from two operations brought on by infection. There, Taft testified before the Senate Committee on the Philippines. Taft was trying to organize an agrarian revolution in the Philippines, he wanted Filipino farmers to have a stake in the new government through land ownership, but much of the arable land was at that time in the hands of Catholic religious orders of mostly Spanish-descended priests, who were often resented by Filipinos. Roosevelt had Taft go to Rome to negotiate with Pope Leo XIII, buy the land and arrange for the removal of the Spanish priests, replacing them with Americans and training the locals as clergy. Taft failed to resolve these problems during his visit to Rome, but in 1903 an agreement was reached on both points.

In late 1902, Taft had heard from Roosevelt that a seat on the Supreme Court would soon become vacant due to the resignation of Justice George Shiras, and Roosevelt wanted Taft to fill the seat. Although this was Taft's career goal, Taft himself declined because he felt his job as governor was not yet finished. The following year, Roosevelt asked Taft to become Secretary of War. While the War Department administered the Philippines, Taft would remain responsible for the islands, and Elihu Root, the incumbent, was willing to postpone his departure until 1904, which gave Taft time to finish his work in Manila. After consulting with his family, Taft agreed and sailed for the United States in December 1903 to accept his appointment.

Secretary of War (1904-1908)

When Taft took over as Secretary of War in January 1904, he was not asked to spend much time administering the military, which the president was content to do himself: Roosevelt wanted Taft as a problem solver in difficult situations, as a legal advisor, and so he could give campaign speeches while seeking election in his own right. Taft vigorously defended Roosevelt's record in his speeches and wrote of the president's successful but energetic efforts to win elections, "I would not run for president if it guaranteed the office. It is horrible to be afraid of one's own shadow."

Between 1905 and 1907, Taft came to terms with the likelihood that he would be the next Republican candidate for president, although he did not plan to actively campaign for it. When Judge Henry Billings Brown resigned in 1906, Taft did not accept the seat even though Roosevelt offered it to him, a position Taft kept when another seat opened up in 1906. Edith Roosevelt, the First Lady , did not like the growing closeness between the two men. She felt they were too much alike and that the president had little to gain from the advice of someone who rarely contradicted him.

Alternatively, Taft wanted to be chief justice and kept a close eye on the health of the elderly incumbent, Melville Fuller , who turned 75 in 1908. Taft believed that Fuller would probably live for many years. Roosevelt had indicated that he would probably appoint Taft if the opportunity arose to fill the court's central post, but some felt that Attorney General Philander Knox was a better candidate. In any event, Fuller remained chief justice during Roosevelt's presidency.

Through Panama's separation from Colombia in 1903 and the Hay-Bunau-Varilla Treaty, the United States had secured the rights to build a canal in the Isthmus of Panama. The legislation authorizing construction did not specify which government department would be responsible, and Roosevelt designated the War Department. Taft traveled to Panama in 1904, saw the canal site, and met with some Panamanian officials. The Isthmian Canal Commission had trouble keeping its chief engineer, and when in February 1907 John F. Stevens resigned, Taft recommended an Army engineer, George W. Goethals. Under Goethals, the project proceeded smoothly.

Another colony lost by Spain in 1898 was Cuba, but since Cuba's freedom had been one of the main objectives of the war, it was not annexed by the United States, but, after a period of occupation, gained independence in 1902, probably due to U.S. fear of the island's mostly Catholic and Hispanic population. In September 1906, President Tomás Estrada Palma requested U.S. intervention. Taft traveled to Cuba with a small U.S. force and on September 29, 1906, under the terms of the 1903 Treaty of Cuban-American Relations, declared himself provisional governor of Cuba, a position he held for two weeks before being succeeded by Charles Eduardo Magon. In his time in Cuba, Taft worked to persuade Cubans that the United States sought stability, not occupation.

Taft remained busy with Philippine affairs. During Roosevelt's election campaign in 1904, he urged that Philippine agricultural products be admitted into the U.S. without tariffs. This caused U.S. sugar and tobacco growers to complain to Roosevelt, who protested to his Secretary of War. Taft expressed his unwillingness to change his position and threatened to resign; Roosevelt hastily dropped the matter. Taft returned to the Philippines in 1905, leading a delegation of U.S. congressmen, and again in 1907, to open the first Philippine Assembly.

On his two trips to the Philippines as Secretary of War, Taft went to Japan and met with officials there. The July 1905 meeting came a month before the Portsmouth Peace Conference, which would end the Russo-Japanese War with the Treaty of Portsmouth. Taft met with Japanese Prime Minister Katsura Tarō. After that meeting, the two signed a memorandum. It contained nothing new, but rather reaffirmed official positions: Japan had no intention of invading the Philippines and the United States that it did not oppose Japanese control of Korea. The United States was concerned about the number of Japanese laborers arriving on the American West Coast, and during Taft's second visit, in September 1907, Tadasu Hayashi , the foreign minister, informally agreed to issue fewer passports for Japanese migrants.

1908 Presidential Elections

Nomination

Roosevelt had served nearly three and a half years of McKinley's term. On the night of his own election in 1904, Roosevelt publicly declared that he would not run for reelection in 1908, a promise he quickly regretted. But he felt bound by his word. Roosevelt believed Taft was his logical successor, although the Secretary of War had initially been reluctant to run. Roosevelt used his control of the party machine to help his heir apparent. On pain of losing their jobs, political appointees were required to support Taft or remain silent.

Several Republican politicians, such as Treasury Secretary George Cortelyou, tested the waters for a run, but opted out. New York Governor Charles Evans Hughes ran, but when he delivered a major policy speech, Roosevelt sent a special message to Congress the same day warning in strong terms against corporate corruption. The resulting coverage of the presidential message relegated Hughes to the back pages. Roosevelt reluctantly discouraged repeated attempts to draft him for another term.

Deputy Postmaster General Frank H. Hitchcock resigned his post in February 1908 to lead Taft's effort. In April, Taft went on a speaking tour, traveling as far west as Omaha before being called upon to straighten out a contested election in Panama. He was seriously unopposed at the 1908 Republican National Convention in Chicago in June and won a victory on the first ballot. However, Taft did not have things his way: he expected his running mate to be a Midwestern progressive like Iowa Senator Jonathan Dolliver, but instead the convention nominated Congressman James S. Sherman of New York, a conservative. Taft resigned as Secretary of War on June 30 to devote full time to the campaign.

General elections

Taft's opponent in the general election was veteran Democratic candidate William Jennings Bryan, the Democratic nominee for the third time in four presidential elections. Since many of Roosevelt's reforms grew out of Bryan's proposals, the Democrat argued that he was the true heir to Roosevelt's mantle. Corporate contributions to federal political campaigns had been prohibited by the Tillman Act of 1907, and Bryan proposed that contributions by corporate officers and directors be similarly prohibited, or at least disclosed when made. Taft was only willing to see contributions disclosed after elections and sought to ensure that officers and directors of corporations that litigated with the government were not among his contributors.

Taft started the campaign on the wrong foot, fueling the arguments of those who said he was not an independent man by traveling to Roosevelt's Sagamore Hill home to receive advice on his acceptance speech, saying he needed "the president's judgment and criticism." Taft supported most of Roosevelt's policies. He argued that workers had the right to organize, but not to boycott, and that corporations and the wealthy should also obey the law. Bryan for his part wanted the railroads to be owned by the government, but Taft advocated that they remain within the private sector, with their maximum rates set by the Interstate Commerce Commission and subject to judicial review. Taft attributed blame for the recent recession, the panic of 1907, to stock market speculation and other abuses, and felt that some currency reform, at that time the United States was under the gold standard, was needed to allow flexibility in government response to bad economic times, that specific trust legislation was needed to supplement the Sherman Antitrust Act, and that the constitution should be amended to allow an income tax, thus overturning Supreme Court decisions striking down such a tax. Roosevelt's expansive use of executive power had been controversial; Taft proposed to continue his policies, but to place them on more solid legal foundations through the passage of legislation.

Taft upset some progressives by choosing Hitchcock as chairman of the Republican National Committee (RNC), putting him in charge of the presidential campaign. Hitchcock was quick to bring in men closely allied with big business. Taft took an August vacation in Hot Springs, Virginia, where he irritated political advisers by spending more time on golf than strategy. After seeing a newspaper photo of Taft taking a big swing at a golf ball, Roosevelt warned him not to take spontaneous shots. Roosevelt, frustrated by his own relative inaction, showered Taft with advice, fearing that the electorate would not appreciate Taft's qualities and that Bryan would win. Roosevelt's supporters spread rumors that the president was running Taft's campaign. This upset Nellie Taft, who never trusted the Roosevelts. However, Roosevelt supported the Republican candidate with such enthusiasm that humorists suggested that "TAFT" stood for "Take Theodore's Advice."

Bryan in his campaign urged a system of bank guarantees, so that depositors could be reimbursed if banks failed, but Taft opposed this and offered instead a postal savings system. The issue of alcohol prohibition entered the campaign when, in mid-September, Carrie Nation called Taft and demanded to know his views. Taft and Roosevelt had agreed that the party platform would take no position on the issue, and Nation left indignantly to claim that Taft was atheistic and anti-religious and against good morals. Taft, following Roosevelt's advice, ignored the issue.

In the end, Taft won by a comfortable margin. Taft defeated Bryan by 321 electoral votes to 162; however, he won only 51.6% of the popular vote. Nellie Taft said regarding the campaign, "There was nothing to criticize, except that he didn't know or care about the way the game of politics is played." Longtime White House usher Ike Hoover recalled that Taft often came to see Roosevelt during the campaign, but rarely between the election and Inauguration Day, March 4, 1909.

Presidency of the United States (1909-1913)

Investiture

The inauguration of William Howard Taft as the twenty-seventh president of the United States took place on Thursday, March 4, 1909, in the Senate chamber inside the United States Capitol, Washington, D. C., instead of the usual East Portico due to a snowstorm. The new president stated in his inaugural address that he had been honored to have been "one of the advisers of my distinguished predecessor" and to have had a part "in the reforms which he has initiated. I should be unfaithful to myself, to my promises, and to the platform statements of the party on which I was elected if I did not make the maintenance and implementation of those reforms a most important feature of my administration." He pledged to make those reforms lasting, ensuring that honest businessmen would not suffer uncertainty from the change in policy. He spoke of the need to reduce the Dingley tariff of 1897, of the need for antitrust reform, and of the Philippines' continued progress toward full self-government. Roosevelt left office regretting that his term in the post he so enjoyed was over and, to get out of Taft's way, he arranged a year-long hunting trip to Africa.

Cabinet

During the 1908 campaign, Taft and Roosevelt had discussed which cabinet members would stay, but Taft kept only Secretary of Agriculture James Wilson and George von Lengerke Meyer. Meyer was moved from the post of postmaster general to the post of secretary of the Navy. Taft also asked Secretary of State Elihu Root to remain in his post, but Root declined and instead recommended former Attorney General Philander C. Knox for the post. Other appointees to Taft's inaugural Cabinet included Secretary of the Interior Richard A. Ballinger, Secretary of the Treasury Franklin MacVeagh, Secretary of War Jacob M. Dickinson, Postmaster General Frank Harris Hitchcock, Secretary of Commerce and Labor Charles Nagel, and Attorney General George W. Wickersham. In 1911, Henry L. Stimson replaced Dickinson and Walter L. Fisher replaced Ballinger.

Throughout his career, Taft identified with the judiciary and made six appointments to the Supreme Court, the most of any president except George Washington and Franklin D. Roosevelt. He appointed Horace H. Lurton in 1909, Charles Evans Hughes, Willis Van Devanter, and Joseph R. Lamar in 1910, and Mahlon Pitney in 1912. In addition, Taft elevated Associate Justice Edward Douglass White to Chief Justice in 1910. The Supreme Court under Chief Justice White proved to be less conservative than previous justices. Three of Taft's appointees left the court in 1917, while Pitney and White remained on the court until the early 1920s. Conservative Van Devanter was the only Taft appointee to serve after 1922, and was part of the Four Horsemen bloc that opposed Franklin D. Roosevelt's New Deal. Taft himself would succeed White as Chief Justice in 1921, and served with Pitney and Van Devanter on the Taft Court.

Taft also appointed 13 judges to the federal courts of appeals and 38 judges to the U.S. district courts. Taft also appointed judges to several specialized courts, including the first five appointees to the U.S. Court of Commerce and the U.S. Court of Customs Appeals.

Vice-Presidency

The vice presidential ticket James S. Sherman had been added to the 1908 Republican ticket as a means of appeasing the conservative wing of the Republican Party, which viewed Taft as a progressive. As Taft moved to the right during his presidency, Sherman emerged as an important ally for the president. Nominated for a second term at the 1912 Republican National Convention , he became ill during the campaign and died on October 30, 1912, just before the election. Because the Constitution lacked a mechanism for choosing an intra-term replacement prior to the ratification of the Twenty-fifth Amendment in 1967, the vice presidency remained vacant for the last 125 days of Taft's presidency. During that time, Secretary of State Philander C. Knox was next in line for the presidency under the U.S. Presidential Succession Act of 1886.

Press corps

Taft did not enjoy the easy relationship with the press that Roosevelt had, choosing not to offer himself for interviews or photo opportunities as often as his predecessor had. His administration marked a shift in style from Roosevelt's charismatic leadership to Taft's calmer passion for the rule of law.

Illness of the first lady

Early in Taft's tenure, in May 1909, his wife Nellie suffered a severe stroke that left her paralyzed in one arm and leg and deprived her of the power of speech. Taft spent several hours each day caring for her and teaching her to speak again, which took a year.

Internal policy

The Taft administration was fraught with conflict between the conservative wing of the Republican Party, with which Taft was often sympathetic, and the progressive wing of the Republican Party, led by Roosevelt and Robert M. La Follette. Controversies over the conservative current and the antitrust cases brought by the Taft administration served to further separate Taft and Roosevelt.

Duties and taxes

Taft sought to reduce tariffs, a tax on imports, which at the time was a major source of government revenue. However, he was outmaneuvered. Taft expanded Roosevelt's efforts to break up the trusts by initiating legal cases against US Steel and other large companies.

Payne-Aldrich Tariff

Immediately after his inauguration, Taft called a special session of Congress to convene in March 1909 to revise the tariffs. The rates had been set by the Dingley Act of 1897 and were the highest in history. The Republican Party had made high tariffs the central pillar of its economic policy since the end of the Civil War, but Taft and some other Republicans had come to believe that the Dingley Act had set the stipends too high. Although the high tariff protected domestic manufacturing, it also hurt U.S. exports and raised the cost of living for the average American. Many saw the tariff as a de facto regressive tax measure on consumers, but it favored policies that would shift the tax burden to corporations and high-income earners. While Roosevelt had largely avoided the tariff issue, Taft became the first Republican president to actively seek to reduce tariffs.

Representative Sereno E. Payne, chairman of the House Ways and Means Committee and an ally of conservative House Speaker Joseph Gurney Cannon, was charged with drafting the tariff legislation. In short, the Payne bill introduced slightly reduced tariffs, but not as much as Taft and progressive Republicans preferred. Payne's bill passed the House in April 1909; when it reached the Senate, the chairman of the Senate Finance Committee, Nelson W. Aldrich, attached numerous amendments raising tariffs. Aldrich's amendments outraged progressives such as Robert M. La Follette of Wisconsin, who strenuously opposed the high rates in the Payne-Aldrich rate bill. Faced with pressure from progressive senators to add an income tax to the bill, Taft and Aldrich arranged for Senator Henry Cabot Lodge to add another amendment to the bill containing a 2% tax on corporate income over $5,000. Following the insertion of that amendment, the bill passed the Senate and went to a conference committee, where minor reductions were made to the tariff rates and the corporate income tax rate was reduced from two percent to one percent. Despite his disappointment with the high tariff rates contained in the final bill, Taft signed the Payne-Aldrich tariff into law.

Despite the inclusion of that tax, the Payne-Aldrich tariff greatly disappointed progressive Republicans, and the resulting disharmony in the Republican Party received widespread exposure in the press, providing Democrats with a powerful campaign issue for the 1910 congressional elections. The divisions within the party that opened up during the tariff debate would plague the Republican Party for the remainder of Taft's presidency.

Sixteenth amendment

During the Payne-Aldrich tariff debate in mid-1909, Congress passed a resolution for a constitutional amendment that would allow the federal government to collect an income tax without having to apportion that tax among the states. The amendment would overturn the Supreme Court's ruling in the 1895 case of *Pollock v. Farmers' Loan & Trust Co.* and thus allow Congress to implement an income tax. An income tax would replace the lost revenue at a lower rate. Passage of the amendment helped appease progressive opponents of the Payne-Aldrich rate and helped ensure that the bill would pass Congress. Conservative leaders in Congress largely opposed actual ratification of the amendment, but believed it had little chance of being ratified, since ratification required approval by three-fourths of state legislatures. Taft himself favored proposing the amendment to state legislatures in large part because he believed that without it a new income tax would undermine the legitimacy of the Supreme Court.

After Congress passed the amendment, conservative Republican leaders, as well as businessmen such as John D. Rockefeller, organized efforts to prevent its ratification. These conservative forces were initially confident that more than a quarter of the state legislature would reject the income tax amendment, but the country shifted in a progressive direction after 1909. Numerous conservative state legislators lost power during the 1910 and 1912 election cycles, and the imposition of taxes in Wisconsin and other states served as evidence of the feasibility of a federal income tax. On February 3, 1913, Wyoming became the 36th state to pass the amendment, and that same month, Secretary of State Knox declared that the United States had ratified the Sixteenth Amendment. After Taft left office, a new federal income tax was imposed through the Revenue Act of 1913.

Antitrust legislation

Taft expanded Roosevelt's efforts to divide the trade combinations through lawsuits filed under the Sherman Antitrust Act, filing 70 cases in four years (Roosevelt had filed 40 in seven years). Lawsuits filed against the Standard Oil Company and the American Tobacco Company, initiated under Roosevelt, were decided in favor of the government by the Supreme Court in 1911. In

June 1911, the Democratic-controlled House of Representatives began hearings on US Steel. Roosevelt had supported US Steel's acquisition of the Tennessee Coal, Iron, and Railroad Company as a means of avoiding the deepening panic of 1907, a decision the former president defended in testimony at the hearings. Taft, as Secretary of War, praised the acquisitions.

In October 1911, Taft's Justice Department filed suit against US Steel, demanding that more than a hundred of its subsidiaries gain corporate independence and naming as defendants many prominent business and financial executives. Taft had not reviewed the pleadings in the case and alleged that Roosevelt "had encouraged monopoly and had been misled by clever industrialists." Roosevelt was offended by the references to him and his administration in the pleadings, and felt that Taft could not evade command responsibility by saying he did not know about them.

Taft sent a special message to Congress on the need for a renewed antitrust statute when it convened its regular session in December 1911, but took no action. Another antitrust case that had political repercussions for Taft was brought against International Harvester Company, the large farm equipment manufacturer, in early 1912. Because the Roosevelt administration had investigated International Harvester but had taken no action, a decision Taft had supported, the suit was caught up in Roosevelt's challenge for the Republican presidential nomination. Taft's supporters alleged that Roosevelt had acted improperly; the former president criticized Taft for waiting three and a half years, and until he was challenged, to reverse a decision he had supported.

Ballinger-Pinchot Controversy

Roosevelt was an ardent conservationist, assisted in this by like-minded appointees, including Secretary of the Interior James R. Garfield and Chief Forester Gifford Pinchot. Taft agreed with the need for conservation, but felt it should be accomplished by legislation rather than executive order. He did not retain Garfield, an Ohio native, as secretary, but chose a Westerner, former Seattle Mayor Richard Ballinger. Roosevelt was surprised by the replacement, believing that Taft had promised to keep Garfield. Roosevelt had withdrawn many lands from the public domain, including some in Alaska that he thought rich in coal. In 1902, Idaho businessman Clarence Cunningham had made mining claims on coal deposits in Alaska, and a government investigation into the matter lasted throughout Roosevelt's presidency. During part of that investigation, Ballinger served as head of the General Land Office. When Ballinger, now Secretary of the Interior, finally approved the claims in 1909, the Land Office agent, Louis Glavis , broke government protocol by leaving the Interior Department to seek help from Pinchot.

In September 1909, Glavis went public with his allegations in a magazine article, revealing that Ballinger had acted as Cunningham's attorney between his two terms of government service. This violated conflict-of-interest rules prohibiting a former government official from advocating a matter for which he had been responsible.On September 13, 1909, Taft dismissed Glavis from government service, based on a report by Attorney General Wickersham dated two days earlier.He also ordered government officials not to comment on the altercation.Pinchot was determined to dramatize the problem by forcing his own dismissal, which Taft tried to avoid, fearing it might provoke a rift with Roosevelt. Taft asked Senator Elihu Root to investigate the matter, and Root urged Pinchot's dismissal.

n January 1910, Pinchot forced the issue by sending a letter to Senator Jonathan Dolliver alleging that, but for the Forest Service's actions, Taft would have approved a fraudulent public land claim. Pinchot was fired and sailed with wounded pride to Europe to make his case to Roosevelt.A congressional investigation followed, which acquitted Ballinger by a majority vote, but the administration was embarrassed when Glavis's attorney, Louis D. Brandeis, proved that Wickersham's report had been retroactive, which Taft belatedly admitted. The Ballinger-Pinchot affair made progressives and Roosevelt loyalists feel that Taft had turned his back on Roosevelt's agenda.

Civil rights

Taft announced in his inaugural address that he would not appoint African Americans to federal jobs, such as postmaster general, when it might cause racial friction. Taft pursued through his policy, the elimination of most blacks as office holders in the South of the country, and made some appointments to that race in the North. Taft vetoed an act passed by Congress and restrained unions from limiting the membership of unskilled workers by imposing a compulsory literacy test.

By the time Taft was inaugurated, its leaders debated the way forward for African Americans. Booker T. Washington felt that most blacks should be trained for industrial work, and only a few would seek higher education; WEB DuBois took a more militant stand for equality. Taft tended to move closer to Washington.

Taft, as a member of the Protestant church of the Unitarian current, was an important leader in the early 20th century of the favorable revaluation of the historical role of Catholicism. He tended to neutralize anti-Catholic sentiments, especially in the Far West, where

Protestantism was a weak force. In 1904, Taft delivered a speech at the University of Notre Dame. He praised the "enterprise, courage, and fidelity to duty which distinguished those heroes of Spain who braved the then frightful perils of the deep to bring Christianity and European civilization to the Philippines." In 1909 he praised Junípero Serra as an "apostle, legislator [and] builder" who fostered "the beginning of civilization in California."

Seventeenth amendment

For the first 125 years of the federal government's existence, Americans did not vote directly for U.S. Senators. The Constitution, as adopted in 1788, provided that senators would be elected by state legislatures. During the 1890s, the House of Representatives passed several resolutions proposing a constitutional amendment for the direct election of senators, but the Senate refused to even vote on such a measure. Several states began calling for a constitutional convention on the issue, as Article V of the U.S. Constitution states that Congress must call a constitutional convention to propose amendments when two-thirds of the state legislatures request one. By 1912, 27 states had called for a constitutional convention on the issue, and 31 states needed to meet the threshold. By April 8, 1913, it had been ratified by the required number of states (36) to become the Seventeenth Amendment to the U.S. Constitution.

States admitted to the union

Since Oklahoma's admission in 1907, there have been 46 states in the union, with the New Mexico Territory and the Arizona Territory being the only territories contiguous to the United States that had not been admitted to the U.S. union. The Enabling Act of 1906 would have allowed Arizona and New Mexico to join the union as a single state, but Arizona voted against the combination in a referendum. In 1910, New Mexico and Arizona wrote a constitution in anticipation of statehood, and Arizona's constitution included progressive ideas such as initiative, referendum, and recall. Taft opposed these mechanisms, particularly the ability to recall judges, and vetoed Arizona's statehood bill. Without such constitutional problems, New Mexico joined the union as the 47th state on January 6, 1912. After Arizona wrote a new constitution that eliminated the power to recall judges, Taft signed a bill admitting Arizona on February 14, 1912. 1912. Arizona then reinstated the recall clause.

Other initiatives

Taft sought greater regulation of railroads and proposed the creation of the U.S. Court of Commerce to hear appeals from the Interstate Commerce Commission (ICC), which provided federal oversight of railroads and other common carriers engaged in interstate commerce. The Mann-Elkins Act established the Court of Commerce and increased the authority of the ICC, placing telephone and telegraph companies under its authority and allowing it to set maximum prices on railroad rates. The Mann-Elkins Act established the Commerce Court and increased the authority of the ICC, placing telephone and telegraph companies under its authority and allowing it to set maximum prices on railroad rates. The Commerce Court proved unpopular with members of Congress and was abolished in 1913.

Taft proposed that the Post Office Department act as a bank that would accept small deposits. Although conservative Republicans opposed the idea, such as Senator Aldrich and House Speaker Joseph Cannon, Taft won passage of a bill establishing the United States Postal Savings System. Taft also oversaw the establishment of a national parcel post delivery system. The results of the 1910 midterm elections were disappointing for the president, as Democrats took control of the House and many of Taft's preferred candidates were defeated. The election was a major victory for progressives in both parties and ultimately helped encourage Roosevelt's third party candidacy in 1912, the so-called Progressive Party. Taft was also disappointed by the defeat of Warren G. Harding in the 1910 Ohio state gubernatorial race, while in New Jersey, Democrat Woodrow Wilson was elected governor. With divided government during the second half of Taft's term, he saw this reduced the passage of far less legislation than in the first half.

Foreign policy

Taft was well educated in foreign affairs, from his academic studies in international arbitration to his administration of the Philippines and especially his service as Secretary of War. His main innovation was to minimize the use of physical power and threats of power, and to emphasize the rapidly growing economic power of the nation. The foreign policy pursued by Secretary of State Philander C. Knox relied on so-called dollar diplomacy to achieve his objectives in Latin America and East Asia through the use of his economic power by encouraging private credits abroad through the guarantee of the U.S. government. The term, originally coined by President Theodore Roosevelt, was used with particular success in Venezuela, Nicaragua, Cuba, China and Liberia. Despite the successes, "dollar diplomacy" could not counteract the economic instability and revolutionary tide in places like Mexico, the Dominican Republic, Nicaragua, and China. Latin Americans have historically disagreed with the role that the U.S. government and U.S. corporations have played in using economic, diplomatic and military power to open foreign markets.

In 1912, President William H. Taft stated regarding his country's foreign policy.

Played a role in China and Latin America. Negotiated a reciprocity treaty for freer trade with Canada, but became entangled in Canadian politics and was rejected. He became completely entangled in domestic politics on the tariff issue, and the result divided his party.

Department of State

Taft gave priority to restructuring the State Department and noted that it was "organized on the basis of the needs of government in 1800 rather than 1900. "The department was for the first time organized into geographic divisions, including desks for the Far East, Latin America, and Western Europe.The department's first in-service training program was established and appointees spent a month in Washington before going to their posts.Taft and Secretary of State Knox had a strong relationship and the president listened to his advice on domestic and foreign affairs. However, Knox was not a good diplomat and had rather difficult relations with the Senate, the press, and many foreign leaders, especially those from Latin America.

There was broad agreement between Taft and Knox on the main foreign policy objectives. The United States would not interfere in European affairs and would use force only if necessary to defend the Monroe Doctrine in the Americas. Defense of the Panama Canal, which was under construction throughout Taft's tenure, guided policy in the Caribbean and Central America. Previous administrations had endeavored to promote U.S. commercial interests abroad, but Taft went a step further and used the network of U.S. diplomats and consuls abroad to promote trade. Such ties, Taft hoped, would promote world peace. Unlike his predecessor, Taft did not seek to arbitrate conflicts between the other great powers. Taft avoided involvement in international events such as the Agadir Crisis, the Italo-Turkish War, and the First Balkan War. However, Taft expressed support for the creation of an international arbitration court and called for an international arms reduction agreement.

Arbitration

Taft favored the resolution of international disputes through arbitration, and in 1911 Taft and Secretary of State Knox negotiated important treaties with Great Britain and France as long as differences were arbitrated. Neither Taft nor Knox consulted with members of the Senate during the negotiation process. By this time, many Republicans opposed Taft and the president felt that pushing too hard for treaties might cause his defeat in the next election. He made some speeches in support of the treaties in October 1911, but the Senate added amendments that Taft could not accept, nullifying the agreements. Roosevelt worked with his close friend, Senator Henry Cabot Lodge, to impose the Senate amendments. Lodge thought the treaties impinged on senatorial prerogatives, while Roosevelt tried to sabotage Taft's campaign promises, also sincerely believed that arbitration was a naive solution and that major problems should be decided by war. Although no general arbitration treaty was concluded, the Taft administration settled several disputes with Great Britain by peaceful means, often with arbitration. These included a boundary settlement between Maine and New Brunswick, a long-running dispute over the Bering Sea seal hunt that also involved Japan, and a similar disagreement over fishing in Newfoundland.

Free trade proposal with Canada

Partly because of the backlash over the high rates of the Payne-Aldrich Tariff, Taft urged the adoption of a free trade agreement with Canada. Britain at that time still managed Canada's foreign relations, and Taft found that the British and Canadian governments were willing to enter into negotiations. Many in Canada opposed an agreement, fearing that the U.S. would scrap it when convenient, as happened with the Elgin-Marcy Treaty in 1866. U.S. agricultural and fishing interests also opposed the treaty. Nevertheless, Taft reached an agreement with Canadian officials in early 1911, and the U.S. Congress approved it in late July. The Canadian parliament, led by Prime Minister Sir Wilfrid Laurier, deadlocked on the issue, and Canadians voted Laurier out of office in the September 1911 election. No cross-border agreement was concluded and the debate deepened divisions in the Republican Party.

Latin America

Taft and Secretary of State Knox instituted a policy of dollar diplomacy toward Latin America, believing that U.S. investment would benefit all concerned and minimize European influence in the area. Although exports increased considerably during the Taft administration, his dollar diplomacy policy was unpopular with Latin American states that did not wish to become financial protectorates of the United States. The Taft administration's foreign policy also faced opposition in the U.S. Senate, as many senators believed that the United States should not interfere abroad.

Mexico

No foreign affairs controversy tested Taft's political skill and commitment to peace more than the collapse of the Mexican regime and the subsequent turmoil of the Mexican Revolution. When Taft took office, Mexico was increasingly unstable under the long dictatorship of Porfirio Díaz. Díaz faced strong political opposition from politician Francisco I Madero, who was backed by a considerable proportion of the population, and also faced serious social unrest provoked by Emiliano Zapata in the south and Pancho Villa in the north. In October 1909, Taft and Díaz exchanged visits across the U.S.-Mexico border, in El Paso, Texas, and Ciudad Juárez, Chihuahua. Their meetings were the first between a U.S. and Mexican president, and also represented the first time a U.S. president had visited Mexico. Díaz hoped to use the meeting as a propaganda tool to show that his government had the unconditional support of the United States. For his part, Taft was primarily interested in protecting U.S. corporate investments in Mexico. The symbolically important meetings helped pave the way for the start of construction of the Elephant Butte Dam project in 1911.

The situation in Mexico deteriorated throughout 1910 and there were a series of incidents in which Mexican rebels crossed the U.S. border to obtain horses and weapons. After Diaz imprisoned opposition candidate Madero prior to the 1910 presidential election, Madero's supporters responded by taking up arms against the government. This unrest resulted in both the overthrow of Diaz and a revolution that would continue for another ten years. In the Arizona Territory, two citizens were killed and nearly a dozen wounded, some as a result of gunfire across the border. Taft would not be incited to fight and therefore instructed the territorial governor not to respond to provocations. In March 1911, he sent 20,000

U.S. troops to the Mexican border to protect U.S. citizens and financial investments in Mexico. Taft told his military aide, Archibald Butt, that "I'm going to sit on the lid and have a hard time getting out."

Nicaragua

In Nicaragua, U.S. diplomats quietly favored the rebel forces of Juan J. Estrada against the government of President José Santos Zelaya, who wanted to revoke trade concessions granted to U.S. companies. Secretary Knox was reportedly a major shareholder in one of the companies that would be harmed by such a move. The country was indebted to several foreign powers, and the United States was unwilling that it and the alternative canal route should fall into the hands of the Europeans. Zelaya and his elected successor, José Madriz, were unable to put down the rebellion, and in August 1910 Estrada's forces took the capital of Managua. The United States made Nicaragua accept a loan and sent officials to make sure it was repaid from government revenues. The country remained unstable, and after another coup in 1911 and more unrest in 1912, Taft sent troops; although most soon withdrew, some remained until 1933.

Panama

Treaties between Panama, Colombia and the United States to resolve disputes arising from the 1903

Panamanian Revolution had been signed by the Roosevelt administration in early 1909, and were approved by the Senate and also ratified by Panama. However, Colombia refused to ratify the treaties and, after the 1912 elections, Knox offered $10 million to the Colombians (later increased to $25 million). The Colombians felt the amount was inadequate and the matter was not resolved under the Taft administration.

Asia

Having served as governor of the Philippines, Taft was very interested in Asian and Pacific affairs. Because of the potential for trade and investment.

China

Taft ranked the post of ambassador to China as the most important in the Foreign Service. Knox disagreed and rejected the suggestion to go to Peking to see the facts on the ground. Taft replaced Roosevelt's ambassador there, William W. Rockhill, as being disinterested in China trade, with William J. Calhoun, whom McKinley and Roosevelt had sent on several foreign missions. Knox did not listen to Calhoun on policy, and there was often conflict. Taft and Knox tried unsuccessfully to extend John Hay's open-door policy to Manchuria. In 1909, a British-led consortium began negotiations to finance a railroad from Hankou to Sichuan. Taft personally appealed to the Prince

Regent, Zaifeng, Prince Chun, and succeeded in obtaining American participation in the railroad financing. However, the Chinese decree authorizing the deal also called for nationalization of local railroad companies in the affected provinces. Inadequate compensation was paid to shareholders, and these grievances were among those that triggered the Chinese Revolution of 1911.

After the revolution broke out, the leaders of the revolt elected Sun Yat-sen as provisional president of what became the Republic of China, overthrowing the Qing dynasty, Taft was reluctant to recognize the new government, although American public opinion was in favor. The U.S. House of Representatives in February 1912 passed a resolution in support of a Chinese republic, but Taft and Knox felt that recognition should be a concerted action by the Western powers. Taft, in his last annual message to Congress in December 1912, indicated that he was moving toward recognition once the republic was fully established, but by then he had been defeated for reelection and did not follow through.

Japan

Taft continued the policy against immigration from China and Japan as under Roosevelt. A revised treaty of friendship and navigation concluded by the U.S. and Japan in 1911 granted extensive reciprocal rights to Japanese in the U.S. and Americans in Japan, but was based on the continuation of the Gentlemen's Agreement. There were objections on the West Coast when the treaty was presented to the Senate, but Taft informed the politicians that there were no changes in immigration policy.

Roosevelt distancing

During Roosevelt's fifteen months of voluntary retirement beyond the Atlantic, from March 1909 to June 1910, neither wrote much to the other. That each waited for the other to take the first step toward reestablishing their relationship on a new basis. After Roosevelt's triumphant return, Taft invited him to stay in the White House. The former president declined and in private letters to friends expressed his dissatisfaction with Taft's performance. However, he wrote that he hoped the Republicans would re-nominate Taft in 1912 and did not speak of himself as a candidate.

Taft and Roosevelt met twice in 1910; the meetings, though outwardly cordial, did not show their former closeness. Roosevelt delivered a series of speeches in the American West in the late summer and early fall of 1910. accused the federal courts of undermining democracy, and called for depriving them of the power to declare legislation unconstitutional . This attack horrified Taft. Roosevelt called for the "elimination of corporate expenditures for political purposes, the physical valuation of railroad property, the regulation of industrial combinations, the establishment of an export tariff commission, a graduated income tax," as well as "labor compensation laws, state and national legislation to regulate the [labor] of women and children, and full advertising of campaign expenditures." According to John Murphy in his magazine article on the rift between the two presidents, "as Roosevelt began to move to the left, Taft veered to the right."

During the 1910 midterm election campaign, Roosevelt became involved in New York state politics, while Taft, with donations and influence, sought to secure the election of the Republican gubernatorial candidate in Ohio, former Lieutenant Governor Warren G. Harding. Republicans suffered losses in the 1910 election when Democrats took control of the House and reduced the Republican majority in the Senate. In New Jersey, Democrat Woodrow Wilson was elected governor and Harding lost his race in Ohio. After the election, Roosevelt continued to promote progressive ideals, a new nationalism, much to Taft's dismay. Roosevelt attacked his successor's administration, arguing that its guiding principles were not those of the party of Lincoln , but those of the Gilded Age. The dispute continued intermittently until 1911, a year in which there were few elections of importance. Wisconsin state senator La Follette announced a presidential candidacy as a Republican and was endorsed by a convention of

Progressives. Roosevelt began taking a position to run in late 1911, and wrote that the tradition that presidents do not run for a third term only applies to consecutive terms.

Roosevelt was receiving many letters from supporters urging him to run, and Republican officials were organizing on his behalf. Hampered by many policies by a reluctant Congress and courts during his full term in the White House, he saw demonstrations of public support that he believed would carry him to the White House with a mandate of progressive policies that would not tolerate opposition. In February, Roosevelt announced that he would accept the Republican nomination if offered. Taft felt that if he lost in November, it would be a repudiation of the party, but if he lost reelection, it would be a repudiation of himself.

1912 Presidential Elections

Nomination

As Roosevelt became more radical in his progressivism,
Taft hardened in his determination to win reelection, as
he was convinced that progressives threatened the very
foundations of government. A blow to Taft was the loss of
Archibald Butt, one of the last links between the previous
and current presidents, as Butt had previously served
Roosevelt. Ambivalent between his loyalties, Butt went
on vacation in Europe and ended up dying in the sinking
of the RMS *Titanic*.

Roosevelt dominated the primaries, winning 278 of the
362 delegates to the Republican National Convention in
Chicago. Taft had control of the party machine, and it was
no surprise that he won most of the decisive delegates at
district or state conventions. Taft did not have a majority,
but was likely to have one once the southern delegations
pledged to him. Roosevelt challenged the election of
these delegates, but the RNC overruled most of the
objections. Roosevelt's only remaining chance was
through a friendly convention chairman, who could make
seating decisions for delegates who favored his side of the

nomination. Taft followed custom and stayed in Washington, but Roosevelt went to Chicago to run his campaign.

Taft had won over Root, who agreed to run for temporary chairman of the convention, and the delegates chose Root over Roosevelt's candidate. Roosevelt's forces moved to substitute delegates who supported for those who argued that they should not be seated. Root made a crucial decision that although the contesting delegates could not vote in their own seats, they could vote in the other contesting delegates, a decision that secured Taft's nomination, as the motion offered by the Roosevelt forces failed. When it became clear that Roosevelt would leave the party if he was not nominated, some Republicans sought a compromise candidate to avoid electoral disaster.Warren Harding placed Taft's name in nomination, whose attempts to praise Taft and unify the party were met with angry interruptions by progressives. Taft was nominated on the first ballot, although most Roosevelt delegates refused to vote.

General Elections

Claiming that Taft had stolen the nomination, Roosevelt and his supporters formed the Progressive Party. Taft knew he would lose, but concluded that through Roosevelt's defeat in Chicago, the party had been preserved as "the defender of conservative government and conservative institutions." He ran his doomed race to preserve conservative control of the Republican Party. Governor Woodrow Wilson was the Democratic nominee. Seeing Roosevelt as the biggest electoral threat, Wilson spent little time attacking Taft, arguing that Roosevelt had been tepid in opposing the trusts during his presidency and that Wilson was the real reformer. Taft contrasted what he called his "progressive conservatism" with Roosevelt's progressive democracy, which to Taft represented "the establishment of a benevolent despotism."

Reverting to the pre-1888 custom that presidents seeking re-election did not campaign, Taft spoke publicly only once and delivered his nomination acceptance speech on August 1. He had early difficulties in financing the campaign, as many industrialists had concluded that he could not win, and that he would therefore support Wilson to block Roosevelt's progressive candidacy. The president issued a confident statement in September after the Republicans narrowly won the Vermont state election in a three-way fight, but he was under no illusions that he would win his race. He had hoped to send his cabinet officials to the campaign trail, but found them reluctant to go. Senator Root agreed to give a single speech for him.

Vice President Sherman had been nominated again in Chicago; seriously ill during the campaign, he died six days before the election, Sherman was the last vice president of the United States to die in office. He was replaced on the ticket by Columbia University president Nicholas Murray Butler. But few voters chose the Taft-Butler ticket, who won only Utah and Vermont, by a total of eight electoral votes. Roosevelt won 88 and Wilson 435. Wilson won with a plurality, not a majority, of the popular vote. Taft finished with just under 3.5 million, more than 600,000 fewer than the former president. Because of voter fraud Taft was not on the ballot in California, due to the actions of local Progressives, nor in South Dakota.

Yale University (1913-1921)

With no pension or other compensation to expect from the government after leaving the White House, Taft contemplated returning to the practice of law, from which he had long been absent. Since Taft had appointed many federal judges, including a majority of the Supreme Court, this would raise questions of conflict of interest at every federal court appearance, and he was saved from this by an offer to become a professor of law and legal history at Yale Law School. He accepted and, after a month's vacation in Georgia, arrived in New Haven on April 1, 1913, to an enthusiastic reception from the university community. Since it was too late in the semester to teach an academic course, he prepared eight lectures on "Questions of Modern Government," which he delivered in May of the same year. He earned money from paid speeches and journal articles, and would finish his eight years out of office by building up his savings. While at Yale, he wrote the treatise *Our Chief Magistrate and His Powers* (1916).

Taft had been appointed chairman of the Lincoln Memorial Commission while still in office; when the

Democrats proposed removing him for one of their party, he joked that, unlike losing the presidency, such a removal would be detrimental. The architect, Henry Bacon, wanted to use Colorado-Yule marble, while Southern Democrats urged the use of Georgia marble. Taft pushed for western stone and the matter was presented to the Commission of Fine Arts, which supported Taft and Bacon. The project went forward; Taft would dedicate the Lincoln Memorial as chief justice of the Supreme Court in 1922. In 1913, Taft was elected to a one-year term as president of the American Bar Association.(ABA), a lawyers' trade group. He removed opponents, such as Louis Brandeis and University of Pennsylvania Law School Dean William Draper Lewis (a Progressive Party supporter), from committees.

Taft maintained a cordial relationship with Wilson. The former president privately criticized his successor on a number of issues, but made his views known publicly only on Philippine policy. Taft was appalled when, after Judge Lamar's death in January 1916, Wilson nominated Brandeis, whom the former president never forgave for his role in the Ballinger-Pinchot affair. When the hearings led to nothing discreditable about Brandeis, Taft intervened with a letter signed by himself and other former ABA presidents, stating that Brandeis was unfit to serve on the Supreme Court. However, the Democratic-controlled Senate confirmed Brandeis. Taft and Roosevelt remained at odds with each other; they met only once in the first three years of Wilson's presidency, at a funeral at Yale. They spoke only for a moment, politely but formally.

As president of the League to Enforce Peace, Taft hoped to avert war through an international association of nations. With World War I in Europe, Taft sent Wilson a note of support for his foreign policy in 1915. President Wilson accepted Taft's invitation to address the league and spoke in May 1916 of a postwar international organization that could prevent a recurrence. Taft supported the effort to get Judge Hughes to resign from office and accept the Republican presidential nomination. Once this was done, Hughes tried to get Roosevelt and Taft to reconcile, as a joint effort was needed to defeat Wilson. This occurred on October 3 in New York, but Roosevelt allowed only a handshake and no words were exchanged. This was one of many difficulties for the Republicans in the campaign, and Wilson narrowly won reelection.

In March 1917, Taft demonstrated public support for the war effort by joining the Connecticut State Guard, a state defense force organized to carry out state functions while the National Guard was on active duty. When Wilson asked Congress to declare war on Germany in April 1917, Taft was an enthusiastic supporter; he was chairman of the executive committee of the American Red Cross, which occupied much of the former president's time. In August 1917, Wilson granted military titles to Red Cross executives as a way of giving them additional authority to use in carrying out their wartime responsibilities, and Taft was appointed major general.

During World War I, Taft took leave from Yale to serve as co-chairman of the National War Labor Board, charged with ensuring good relations between the owners of industry and their workers. In February 1918, the new chairman of the RNC, Will H. Hays , approached Taft seeking his reconciliation with Roosevelt. While at the Palmer House in Chicago, Taft heard that Roosevelt was dining there, and after he entered, the two men embraced to the applause of the room, but the relationship did not progress; Roosevelt died in January 1919. Taft later wrote: "Had he died in a hostile state of mind toward me, I would have mourned the fact all my life. I always loved him and treasure his memory."

When Wilson proposed the establishment of a League of Nations, Taft expressed his public support. He was the leader of the activist wing of his party and was opposed by a small group of senators who strongly opposed the League. Taft's reversal on whether reservations on the Treaty of Versailles were necessary angered both parties, prompting some Republicans to call him a supporter of

Wilson and a traitor to his party. The Senate refused to ratify the Versailles pact.

Chief Justice of the Supreme Court (1921-1930)

During the 1920 election campaign, Taft supported the Republican candidacy of Warren G. Harding, then a senator, and Massachusetts Governor Calvin Coolidge; they were elected. Taft was among those invited to go to the president-elect's home in Marion, Ohio, to advise him on appointments, and the two men consulted there on December 24, 1920. According to Taft's later account, after a conversation, Harding casually asked if Taft would accept the Supreme Court appointment; if Taft would, Harding would appoint him. Taft had a condition for Harding: having served as chief justice and having appointed two of the current associate justices and opposed Brandeis, he could only accept the chief justice position. Harding did not respond, and Taft in a thank-you note reiterated the condition and stated that Chief Justice White had often told him that he would hold Taft's seat until a Republican occupied the White House. In January 1921, Taft heard through intermediaries that Harding planned to appoint him, if he had the opportunity.

By then, White was in failing health, but he made no move to resign when Harding was sworn in on March 4, 1921. Taft visited the chief justice on March 26 and found White ill, but he was still continuing his work and did not talk about retiring. White did not retire, dying in office on May 19, 1921. Taft paid tribute to the man he had appointed to the center seat and waited and worried whether he would be White's successor. Despite widespread speculation that Taft would be the choice, Harding did not make a quick announcement. Taft was lobbying for himself behind the scenes, especially with Ohio politicians who formed Harding's inner circle.

It was later learned that Harding had also promised former Utah Senator George Sutherland a seat on the Supreme Court and hoped that another seat would become vacant. Harding was also considering a proposal by Justice William R. Day to crown his career by being chief justice for six months before retiring. Taft felt, when he learned of this plan, that a short-term appointment would not be good for the position and that, once confirmed by the Senate, Day's memory would be darkened. After Harding rejected Day's plan, Attorney General Harry Daugherty, who supported Taft's candidacy, urged him to fill the vacancy and appointed Taft as president on June 30, 1921. The Senate confirmed Taft the same day, 61-4, without any committee hearing and after a brief debate in executive session. Taft drew objections from three progressive Republicans and one Southern Democrat, the Republicans being Hiram Johnson of California, William E. Borah of Idaho, and La Follette of Wisconsin. The Democrat was Thomas E. Watson of Georgia. When he was sworn in on July 11, he became the first and to date only person to serve as both President of the United States and Chief Justice of the U.S. Supreme Court.

Trade clause

The Supreme Court under Taft compiled a conservative record on Commerce Clause jurisprudence. This had the practical effect of making it difficult for the federal government to regulate the industry, and the Taft Court also struck down many state laws. Congress attempted to end child labor by imposing a tax on certain corporations that made use of it. That law was struck down by the Supreme Court in 1922 in *Bailey v. Drexel Furniture Co.* and Taft wrote the court's opinion for a majority of 8 to 1. It held that the tax was not intended to raise revenue, but was an attempt to regulate matters reserved to the states under the Tenth Amendment, and that allowing such a tax would remove power from the states. One case in which Taft and his court upheld federal regulation was *Stafford v. Wallace*. Taft ruled by a 7-1 majority that the processing of animals in stockyards was so closely related to interstate commerce as to bring it within the scope of Congress's regulatory power.

One case in which the Taft Court struck down regulation that generated a dissent by the Chief Justice was *Adkins v. Children's Hospital*. Congress had enacted a minimum wage for women in the District of Columbia. A 5-3 majority of the Supreme Court struck it down. Justice Sutherland wrote for the majority that the recently ratified Nineteenth Amendment, guaranteeing women the vote, meant that the sexes were equal in bargaining power over working conditions; Taft, dissenting, found this unrealistic. Taft's dissent in *Adkins* was rare both because he authored few dissents and because it was one of the few times he took an expansive view of the government's police power.

Powers of the government

In 1922, Taft ruled unanimously in *Balzac v. Porto Rico*, *Balzac* involved a Puerto Rico newspaper publisher who was prosecuted for libel but denied a jury trial, a Sixth Amendment protection under the constitution. Taft held that since Puerto Rico was not a territory designated for statehood, only constitutional protections enacted by Congress would apply to its residents.

In 1926, Taft wrote for a 6-3 majority in *Myers v. United States*, that Congress could not require the president to obtain Senate approval before removing an appointee. Taft pointed out that there is no restriction on the president's power to remove officials in the Constitution. Although *Myers* involved the removal of a postmaster general, Taft, in his opinion, held invalid the repealed Tenure of Office Act , for the violation of which his presidential predecessor, Andrew Johnson , had been indicted, although acquitted by the Senate.

The following year, the court decided *McGrain v. Daugherty.* A congressional committee investigating former Attorney General Daugherty's possible complicity in the Teapot Dome scandal requested records from his brother, Mally, who refused to provide them, claiming that Congress had no power to obtain documents from him. Van Devanter ruled in favor of a unanimous court against him and found that Congress had the authority to conduct investigations as ancillary to its legislative function.

Individual and civil rights

In 1925, the Taft Court laid the groundwork for the incorporation of many of the Bill of Rights guarantees that would be enforced against the states through the Fourteenth Amendment. In *Gitlow v. New York,* the Court, by a 6-2 vote with Taft in the majority, upheld Gitlow's conviction on charges of criminal anarchy for advocating the overthrow of the government; his defense was freedom of speech. Judge Edward T. Sanford wrote the opinion of the Court, and both the majority and minority assumed that the First Amendment's Freedom of Speech and Freedom of the Press clauses were protected against infringement by the states.

Pierce v. Society of Sisters was a 1925 decision by the Taft Court that struck down an Oregon law banning private schools. In a decision written by Judge James C. McReynolds, a unanimous court held that Oregon could regulate private schools, but not eliminate them. The result upheld the right of parents to control their children's education, but also, since the lead plaintiff (the society) ran Catholic schools, dealt a blow to religious freedom.

United States v. Lanza was one of a series of cases involving alcohol prohibition. Lanza committed acts allegedly in violation of state and federal law, and was first convicted in a Washington state court and then prosecuted in federal district court. He alleged that the second indictment violated the double jeopardy clause of the Fifth Amendment. Taft, by a unanimous vote of the court, allowed the second prosecution, holding that the state and federal governments were dual sovereigns, each empowered to prosecute the conduct at issue.

In the 1927 case *Lum v. Rice*, Taft wrote for a unanimous Court that included liberals Holmes, Brandeis, and Stone.

The ruling held that the exclusion on the basis of race of a child of Chinese descent from an all-white public school did not violate the Fourteenth Amendment to the U.S. Constitution. This allowed states to extend segregation in public schools to Chinese students.

Political influence

Taft exercised the power of his office to influence the decisions of his colleagues, urging unanimity and discouraging dissent. Alpheus Mason, in his article on Chief Justice Taft for the *American Bar Association Journal*, contrasted Taft's expansive view of the Chief Justice's role with the narrow view of presidential power he assumed while in that office. Taft saw nothing wrong with making his views on potential appointments to the Court known to the White House, and he resented being criticized in the press. He was initially a strong supporter of President Coolidge after Harding's death in 1923, but became disillusioned with Coolidge's appointments. Taft advised Republican presidents in office while he was chief justice to avoid "out-of-touch" appointees such as Brandeis and Holmes.

Believing that the Chief Justice should be responsible for the federal courts, Taft felt that he should have an administrative staff to assist him, and that the Chief Justice should be empowered to temporarily reassign judges. When Congress met in December 1921, a bill was introduced for 24 new judges, to empower the Chief Justice to move judges temporarily to eliminate delays and to preside over a body composed of the senior appellate judge of each circuit. Congress objected to some aspects, requiring Taft to obtain the agreement of the senior judge of each circuit involved before assigning a judge, but passed the bill in September 1922 and the Judicial Conference of Senior Circuit Judges held its first meeting that December.

When Taft became Chief Justice, the Court did not have its own building and met in the Capitol. Its offices were cluttered and overcrowded, but Fuller and White had opposed proposals to move the Court to its own building. In 1925, Taft began a fight to get a building for the Court, and two years later, Congress appropriated money to buy the land, on the south side of the Capitol. Cass Gilbert had prepared plans for the building and was hired by the government as an architect. Taft expected the Court to move into the new building, but it did not do so until 1935, after Taft's death.

Death

Taft is remembered as the heaviest president in U.S. history; he was 5 feet 11 inches (6 feet 11 m) tall and his weight peaked at 335 to 340 pounds (152 to 154 kg) toward the end of his presidency, When Taft became chief justice in 1921, his health was beginning to deteriorate and he carefully planned an exercise regimen, walking 3 miles (4.8 km) from his home to the Capitol every day. When he returned, he usually went along Connecticut Avenue and used a particular crossing over Rock Creek. After his death, the crossing was named the Taft Bridge.

His health gradually deteriorated during his nearly decade-long tenure as chief justice. Worried that if he retired, his replacement would be chosen by President Herbert Hoover, whom he considered too progressive, he wrote to his brother Horace in 1929: "I am older and slower, less sharp and more confused. However, as long as things continue as they are, and I can answer in my place, I must stay on the court to prevent the Bolsheviks from taking over."

Taft insisted on going to Cincinnati to attend the funeral of his brother Charles, who died on December 31, 1929; the strain did not improve his own health. When the court reconvened on January 6, 1930, Taft had not returned to Washington, and Van Devanter issued two opinions that Taft had drafted but had been unable to complete because of his illness. Taft went to Asheville, North Carolina , to rest, but by late January he could barely speak and was hallucinating.Taft feared that Stone would be appointed chief justice; he did not resign until Hoover assured him that he would choose Charles Evans Hughes. Taft resigned as chief justice on February 3, 1930. Returning to Washington after his resignation, Taft was barely physically or emotionally strong enough to sign a response to a letter of tribute from the eight associate justices. He died at his home in Washington, D. C., on March 8, 1930, at age 72, probably of heart disease, liver inflammation, and high blood pressure.

Taft was laid to rest in the rotunda of the U.S. Capitol. On March 11, he became the first president and first member of the Supreme Court to be buried at Arlington National Cemetery in Virginia.

Other books by United Library

https://campsite.bio/unitedlibrary